AF220574

100 reasons to have sex

a Sexologist's Enumeration

100 reasons to have sex

a Sexologist's Enumeration

Lara Flamme

Bibliografische Information der Deutschen Nationalbibliothek: Die Deutsche Nationalbibliothek verzeichnet diese Publikation in der Deutschen Nationalbibliografie; detaillierte bibliografische Daten sind im Internet über dnb.dnb.de abrufbar

© 2020 Lara Flamme

Herstellung und Verlag: BoD – Books on Demand, Norderstedt

ISBN: 9783752610512

Sex is the basis for our existence. If we didn't have sex, none of us would be alive.

Although biologically, sexual reproduction is the primary reason humanity has sex, we have given sex so much more meaning...

Before we start, I want to thank anyone who has ever pleased me sexually.

Also thank you for being creative and funny with me, Will.
To Marcel, Ryan and Marc, thanks for being my most reliable proofreaders.

1: To experience your body consciously

2: For relieving stress

3: For fun

4: Because you can

5: To end an argument

6: To start an argument

7: To let go of anger
in a healthy way

8: To make a baby

9: ... or two

10: To get you ready
for the day

11: To feel more connected to your partner

12: To burn calories

13: To make up

14: Because you're bored

15: To boost your immune system

16: To fall asleep more easily

17: So you can smoke a cigarette after sex

18: To experience your femininity

19: To experience your masculinity

20: To rid yourself of any kind of pain

21: To discover your sexual preferences

22: To feel better
about yourself

23: To experience the beautiful things in life

24: To be creative

25: To get some stretching done

26: To seek revenge

27: As an act of gratitude

28: To keep your partner from straying

29: To feel loved

30: To give love

31: To make money

32: To satisfy your sex drive

33: To fight depression

34: To be in the moment

35: To feel your
partner orgasm

36: To do something even more interesting than self-pleasure

37: To be more comfortable with someone

38: To try all the positions in the Kama Sutra

39: To keep yourself warm in winter

40: ... and hot in summer

41: To make time pass more quickly (but not too quickly, if you know what I mean...)

42: To feel desired

43: To fall in love without having to ask The 36 Questions that Lead to Love

44: Because you're hungry, but not for food

45: To keep your marriage

46: ... or to end it (I hope not!)

47: To have an excuse to stay in bed longer

48: To keep your vagina flexible and hydrated

49: To improve your
sexual skills

50: To gain an advantage

51: To find out what you really feel for someone

52: To have more exciting stories to put in your journal

53: To make someone jealous

54: To act out a sexual fantasy you've been dreaming about

55: To feel young (again)

56: To feel grownup

57: To get over someone

58: To fall in love

59: To fall out of love

60: To keep up the routine

61: To celebrate life

62: To celebrate
anything else

63: To experience the wonder of orgasm

64: For two to become one

65: To be more focused afterwards

66: Because you're horny

67: To thank your partner for being amazing

68: To remind your partner that you are a sexual being

69: To try out this number

70: To make the shower afterwards more worth it

71: To forget your problems

72: To help your partner forget their problems

73: To communicate
with your partner

74: To figure out your sexual orientation

75: To be happy

76: To boost your libido

77: As a substitute for coffee in the morning

78: To become better at it

79: To be vulnerable

80: To make things better

...or worse

81: To climax
together

82: To feel goosebumps

83: To show your partner what you like

84: To leave love bites

85: To find your boundaries (and to learn to break them?)

86: To feel alive

87: To take control

88: To let yourself be controlled

89: To smell your partner's bodily fluids

90: To feel a little naughty without doing anything wrong

91: To go on an adventure without leaving town

92: To elongate your life

93: To save some of your make up because your face will glow without it

94: To enjoy being naked

95: To release hormones for lust, attraction, satisfaction and attachment

96: To re-enact a (porn?) scene that you like

97: To make good use
of your really big
hotel bed, shower
and balcony

98: To get the butterflies in your stomach flying

99: To erupt with joy

100: To give this book validation